CONTENTS

Where on Earth are rivers?

LUCKY LANDING
In 2009, a US pilot managed to land safely in the Hudson river after his plane was hit by birds.

COLORADO RIVER

MISSISSIPPI RIVER

WHOOSH!
Imagine turning **800 MILLION** bath taps on full. That's how much water rushes out of the Amazon river into the Atlantic Ocean!

Is there a river somewhere near you? The answer is probably yes! Rivers flow on every continent, across almost any type of land. In some places you only see them during a rainy season, or in an extra-wet year. Rivers need plenty of water – and a slope to rush or trickle down.

Rivers are useful to us in all sorts of ways, from drinking to transport and power. In this book you'll discover WHERE, HOW and WHY ON EARTH rivers are so important!

All rivers have a mouth. Not for eating with – it's where they flow out into a lake or the sea.

They also have a basin – that's all the surrounding land that drains into them.

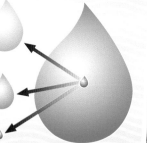

SALT v FRESH

Saltwater 97.5%

Freshwater 2.5%

68.9% ice and snow

30.8% groundwater

0.3% lakes and rivers

WORLD WATER
If you put all the world's water in a bath, only a tiny drop would be river water.

GULP!

Many major cities are built by rivers. More than 7 million people in London get their drinking water from the River Thames.

WATCH OUT!

Europe's busiest river is the Rhine.

DANUBE

FREE FISH

On the Mekong river, some people live in stilt houses and catch fish through traps in the floor!

NILE

RIVER DEEP

The Congo is the world's deepest river – it's a 230m swim to the bottom in some parts.

FERTILE LAND

Farmers in Australia rely on the Murray and Darling rivers to irrigate their land.

USING RIVERS

We each use an average of 150 litres of water a day – and a lot of that comes from rivers. It takes:

 80 LITRES FOR A BATH

 50 LITRES FOR A WASHING MACHINE CYCLE

 12 LITRES PER MINUTE FOR A POWER SHOWER

 14,000 LITRES TO PRODUCE A KILOGRAM OF BEEF

 2,700 LITRES TO MAKE A T-SHIRT

 70 LITRES TO GROW AN APPLE

Where can you find prehistoric water?

Amazingly, all the water in the world today has been around for billions of years – since dinosaur times and before. So next time you kayak down a river or even turn on a tap, you could be dabbling in the same water as T. rex! OK, it's been recycled a few times...

THE AVERAGE RIVER WOULD DRY UP WITHIN WEEKS WITHOUT TOP-UPS FROM RAIN AND GROUNDWATER.

Earth's water is always on the move. It flows from rivers to the sea, falls as rain and runs off the land or seeps underground. On top of all that, it keeps changing state (sometimes it doesn't even look like water!). If it's cold enough, water freezes to ice, and when things heat up, it evaporates into the air. All this moving and changing of water is called the water cycle.

WE CAN'T MAKE WATER. THERE'S THE SAME AMOUNT ON EARTH TODAY AS THERE WAS WHEN THE PLANET WAS FORMED.

NOTES ON WATER

FOSSIL WATER

Underground water stores, called aquifers, can stay there for thousands of years. Really old groundwater is known as fossil water.

SWEATY PLANTS

Plants take in water – and they also 'sweat' it out. This process is called transpiration. A square metre of cornfield gives off about 4 litres of water each day. In a year, a big tree can transpire thousands of litres!

Lots of water is stored as snow and ice.

Water vapour cools and condenses, forming clouds.

Heavy clouds release rain, hail or snow.

Some water sinks underground.

Water runs off land into lakes, rivers and oceans.

The Sun's heat makes surface water evaporate.

25221. Neg 34455

CIRCUIT SPEEDS

A water molecule hangs around in a cloud for about ten days before falling as rain.

Water can take days, weeks or months to get down a river (some rivers flow faster than others).

Groundwater moves far slower than surface water – by as little as a metre a day or even a year or decade. A snail can manage a metre in an hour!

Currents under the oceans circulate water around the world – the full loop can take 1,000 years!

Drop To Drink

We recycle water too. A drop of rain falling into the Thames river at its source will have been drunk by eight people before it reaches the sea (don't worry, it gets cleaned in between!).

How long would it take to swim the River Nile?

You'd need a lot of puff – the **Nile** measures 6,670 km! If you swam at 4 km/hr, for 8 hours a day, it could take 7 **MONTHS** to get that far. There are deadly crocodiles lurking in the water, and you'd slow right down if you went against the current...

A satellite image of just part of the vast river Nile

We don't recommend you try it – even to say you've conquered the LONGEST RIVER IN THE WORLD!

Measuring rivers isn't easy. First you have to work out where they start. Finding the source of the Nile baffled explorers for centuries. The river has two main channels – the Blue Nile and the White Nile. It's the White Nile that gives it its record-breaking length.

The White Nile flows from a huge African lake – Lake Victoria. But smaller rivers feed into the lake, so where is the true source? People still disagree whether it's a spring in Burundi or Rwanda. The Blue Nile starts in Ethiopia, meeting the White Nile in Sudan. Before it reaches the Mediterranean Sea, the river splits into smaller channels.

NOTES ON THE NILE

INTERNATIONAL WATERS

The Nile basin includes 11 countries: Kenya, Eritrea, the Democratic Republic of the Congo, Burundi, Uganda, Tanzania, Rwanda, Egypt, Sudan, South Sudan and Ethiopia. The river drains a tenth of the land in Africa!

Busy River

Around 160 million people depend on the Nile for their water supply and to irrigate crops. In Egypt, at least 95% of the population lives close to the river.

Travel Bug

In 1858, English explorer John Hanning Speke traced the Nile to Lake Victoria - but only after suffering various horrors, including going deaf for a while when a beetle got buried in his ear!

SWIMMING CHAMP

Martin Strel, a Slovenian who is famous for swimming the length of rivers, took 66 days to conquer the Amazon (5,268 km of it) in 2007. He's also swum the Mississippi, the Danube and the Yangtze - but not the Nile!

TOP 3 LONGEST RIVERS

1 ......

2

3

Nile (Africa) 6,670 km

Amazon (South America) 6,404 km

Yangtze (Asia) 6,378 km

Lake Victoria

LAKE VICTORIA WAS NAMED AFTER THE GREAT BRITISH QUEEN.

Queen Victoria

How many swimming pools could a waterfall fill?

In the case of Iguaçu Falls in South America... 300 in a minute! At the height of the rainy season it hurls 13 million litres of water – five Olympic pools – PER SECOND into the Devil's Throat (that's a gorge at the bottom, not an evil body part).

This massive waterfall is part of the Iguaçu river, which tumbles over the edge of a plateau on the border of Brazil and Argentina. It's actually made up of 275 separate falls, broken by rocks and islands. In total, Iguaçu Falls is 2.7 km wide and varies in height up to 82m.

In June 2014, heavy rains sent a record 46 million litres (18 Olympic pools) per second crashing over Iguaçu! Not surprisingly, this caused a lot of damage to surrounding areas. At less ferocious times, visitors can admire the cascades from special walkways, a helicopter or a boat.

THE WORD 'IGUAÇU' LITERALLY TRANSLATES AS 'BIG WATER'!

WATERFALL NOTES

Tallest

Angel Falls (in Venezuela) is so tall that in hot weather the water turns to mist before reaching the bottom. At 979m, it's nearly 20 times higher than Niagara (52m) and taller than three Eiffel Towers!

WIDEST

Khone Falls (in Laos) is a series of falls and rapids more than 10 km (10,783m, to be precise) from edge to edge.

In 2012, Nik Wallenda crossed Niagara Falls from the USA to Canada – on a tightrope! In 2013, he took it one step (actually, a lot of steps) further and crossed the Grand Canyon (see p16).

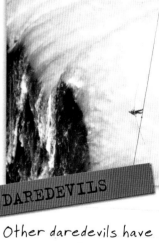

BIGGEST CURTAIN OF FALLING WATER

The cascade at Victoria Falls (in Zimbabwe/Zambia) is 1,700m wide and 80–108m high – an area bigger than 600 tennis courts! The local name for Victoria Falls is 'the smoke that thunders'. The 'smoke' is actually water spray!

MOST VISITED WATERFALL

Niagara Falls (in the USA/Canada) isn't the biggest or the most powerful. But it is the most visited waterfall in the world, attracting more than 20 million tourists a year.

DAREDEVILS

Other daredevils have gone over Niagara Falls in a barrel. Not all have survived.

YOU CAN HEAR THE ROAR OF IGUAÇU'S WATER SEVERAL KILOMETRES AWAY!

Which river carries the most water?

The Amazon narrowly misses being the world's longest river, but it definitely takes first prize for holding the most water. A fifth of all river water on the planet rushes along it – more than the next five biggest rivers combined!

THE AMAZON IS SO HUGE, IT'S OFTEN CALLED 'THE RIVER SEA'!

AMAZON NOTES

THE RIVER SHOOTS A PLUME OF FRESH WATER ABOUT 400 KM INTO THE OCEAN.

The Amazon flows across South America, from mountains in Peru to the Atlantic Ocean. More than 1,100 tributaries pour into it along its course. Together they drain an area more than twice the size of India, making up the biggest river basin on Earth. Most of the water they collect comes from the Amazon rainforest.

It's a bad idea to snooze on the banks of the Amazon – there are flesh-eating creatures around! In the rainy season, there's also a risk you'll get washed away. The river rises by up to 20m and floods vast stretches of forest. At its widest, the channel can swell from 10 km to 48 km across!

Mighty Mouth

The mouth of the Amazon measures over 325 km across - more than the English Channel at its widest point! It's home to an island about the size of Switzerland, called Marajó.

Every minute the Amazon empties 13 billion litres of water into the ocean - enough to supply everyone in London for several days. During the rainy season it could fill 120 Olympic pools in a second (making Iguaçu Falls look quite tame)!

ROARING WAVE

Twice a year during very high tides, a giant wave ROARS up the Amazon from the sea. Nicknamed the pororoca (meaning 'great destructive noise'), it reaches up to 4m high. Surfers love it!

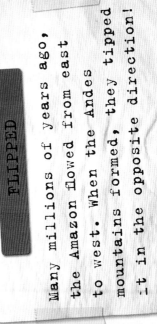

FREAKY FISH

The Amazon is home to at least 2,500 types of fish - more than all of Europe's rivers put together! They include electric eels, razor-toothed piranhas and the pirarucu, one of the largest freshwater fish in the world.

FLIPPED

Many millions of years ago, the Amazon flowed from east to west. When the Andes mountains formed, they tipped it in the opposite direction!

How can rivers wear down mountains?

Every day, rivers dump about 55 MILLION tonnes of rock, mud and sand into the sea (not all in the same place – that would make one gigantic splash!). They get all this stuff from the land they flow through, including mighty mountains...

VALLEYS

Rivers have the power to carve valleys into hills and mountains. V-shaped valleys form near the start of a river, where the water is fast and furious.

When water rushes over soil or even rock, it takes little (or sometimes big) pieces with it. These pieces help to bash and grind at the riverbed and banks. Bit by bit, sometimes over millions of years, the ground gets whittled away. This Earth-shaping action is called erosion.

OLD AGE

A river starts fast and narrow, then gets wider and more sluggish as it nears its end.

SOME VALLEYS HAVE BEEN WIDENED BY GLACIERS – HUGE, SLOW-MOVING RIVERS OF ICE.

RIVER RUBBLE

The world's rivers dump the weight of seven Empire State Buildings in the sea every hour!

Rivers need somewhere to drop all the rubble they've picked up. If they do this before they reach the sea, they can slowly change their own path.

MEANDERING EXPLAINED

Loopy meanders like these form on gentle slopes in the middle section of rivers.

The river strips land from outer bends, where the flow is strongest...

...and dumps it on inner bends, where the flow is weaker.

The flat land either side of a river is called its floodplain.

25221. Neg 34455

NOTES ON DELTAS

When rivers reach the sea, they have nowhere else to put stuff! Sometimes the tide sweeps sediment away - otherwise it builds up to form a delta.

DELTA FACTS

The Ganges delta in India and Bangladesh is the largest in the world. Covering about 100,000 sq km, it's almost as big as Iceland.

Over centuries, China's Huang He delta has moved up and down the coast as the river has changed its course!

The Mississippi, USA, carries over a million tonnes of sediment to its delta each day.

River deltas

How deep is the Grand Canyon?

Picture a drop so deep you could dangle FIVE-AND-A-HALF Eiffel Towers end-to-end! The Grand Canyon, USA, measures a dizzying 1.8 km from top to bottom. It's not actually the deepest gully in the world – but you wouldn't want to trip over the edge.

How did the canyon form? Largely thanks to the Colorado river. Over 6 million years it has carved its way through the landscape, cutting further and further through ancient layers of rock. Wind, rain and ice have worn away at the canyon walls too, adding to the dramatic scenery.

Looking into the canyon is like a trip through time – the rock at the bottom is nearly 2 BILLION years old. At the top it's much younger, at 230 million years old (still, it's been around since the first dinosaurs!). You can clearly see the layers of history as multicoloured stripes in the rock.

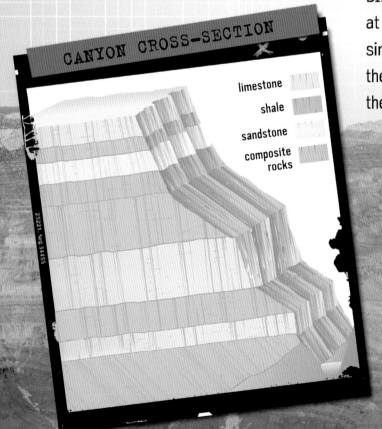

CANYON CROSS-SECTION

limestone

shale

sandstone

composite rocks

25221 NR 34455

FOSSILS OF ANCIENT ANIMALS APPEAR IN THE GRAND CANYON'S ROCK.

CANYON NOTES

PEOPLE PIT

If you piled every person on Earth into the Grand Canyon, they would only take up a tiny part of it. Even all the people who have ever lived (around 107 billion) could jump in with room to spare!

HOME

Native Americans have lived in and around the Grand Canyon for thousands of years. The Paiute tribe call the canyon 'Kaibab', meaning 'mountain lying down'!

OUT OF THIS WORLD!

You can see the Grand Canyon from space, where in fact there's a far bigger one. Valles Marineris on Mars is almost 10 times longer and 4 times deeper! If it were on Earth, it would stretch right across the USA.

DEEPER

Cotahuasi Canyon in Peru is about twice as deep as the Grand Canyon. Yarlung Tsangpo in China (pictured) is more than three times as deep at its lowest point – you could stack 18 Eiffel Towers there!

LONG HIKE

Watch out for rattlesnakes, like this one!

The Grand Canyon is 446 km long and 29 km wide at its furthest points. To walk across it you need two or three days, lots of water and an eye out for snakes and scorpions.

WIDER

Australia's Capertee Valley is 30 km wide, just pipping the Grand Canyon.

THE COLORADO RIVER SUPPLIES WATER TO 30 MILLION PEOPLE IN SEVEN US STATES.

Which river is a lifeline to more than 450 million people?

450 million is over seven times the population of the UK! But in India and Bangladesh, this many people and more rely on one river – the Ganges. They use its water for farming, fishing, industry, transport, washing, drinking and even praying.

For an important river, the Ganges isn't that long. At 2,510 km, it is less than half the length of the Nile. But more people count on it than any other river in the world. Thousands of villages, towns and cities are built along its course. About 1 in 14 people on the planet live in the Ganges basin!

BIG BASIN FACTS

⭐ 1,200 BILLION cubic metres of rain fall yearly in the Ganges basin

⭐ 500 MILLION people live there (approximately)

⭐ 1 MILLION square kilometres are drained by the basin

⭐ 550 is the average number of people per square kilometre

WATER OF LIFE

The Ganges provides water for crops such as rice, oilseed, lentils, tea, sugarcane, wheat, cotton, jute and more! More than 7 in 10 people in India and about half the population of Bangladesh are involved in farming.

IT TAKES 3,400 LITRES OF WATER TO PRODUCE A KILOGRAM OF RICE.

LOCALS CALL THE RIVER 'GANGA MA' OR MOTHER GANGES.

GANGES NOTES

A PLACE TO PRAY

The Ganges is sacred to Hindus – about a billion people around the world. According to their faith, the river is a goddess and can cleanse away sins.

Kumbh Mela is the world's largest river festival – 120 million pilgrims rush to bathe and pray in a single place on the Ganges.

Even after death, Hindus rely on the goddess Ganga. Ashes from hundreds of riverside cremations are scattered in the water every day.

The Ganges flows from the Himalayan mountains, through India and Bangladesh to the Bay of Bengal. Here, with the help of other rivers, it has built up a massive delta. This is the place to be for fertile soil and farming – it's one of the most densely populated places on Earth.

MILLIONS OF PEOPLE SWIM AND BATHE IN THE RIVER EVERY DAY.

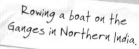
The Ganges delta has very fertile soil for growing crops, including rice.

Rowing a boat on the Ganges in Northern India.

POLLUTION

As it flows past cities, farms and factories, the Ganges collects dangerous amounts of waste. A few things that get dumped in it daily are:

★ Raw sewage - about a billion litres

★ Industrial waste - about 260 million litres

★ Runoff from fertilisers and pesticides

★ Animal carcasses and human remains

In one attempt to clean up the Ganges, thousands of flesh-eating turtles were let loose in the water!

The river Ganges starts its journey high up in the Himalayan mountains.

Which river creatures spell DANGER?

Out at sea you might expect to run into (or away from) a man-eating shark. But rivers? Yes, sharks live in rivers too! In fact rivers are home to a whole range of freshwater frights – be careful where you paddle.

Rivers support huge ecosystems, from microscopic organisms to humungous hippos. Many plants and animals have adapted to survive extreme conditions, such as waterfalls and murky mud. Altogether, about 126,000 species live in the world's fresh water. It's a case of 'eat your neighbours' to get by!

NIPPERS

DIVING BELL SPIDERS are the only spiders that can live underwater. Nifty trick: they surround themselves in a bubble-like web so they can breath air. Nasty trick: they bite, and can bring on a fever.

GNASHERS

PIRANHAS are armed with razor-sharp teeth and a mighty appetite for meat. They can strip flesh off a bone in seconds.

WRIGGLERS

The CANDIRU is a small, narrow and greatly feared catfish. It can swim into all sorts of teeny passages, including the urethra (the tube you wee out of).

'PIRANHA' COMES FROM A NATIVE AMERICAN WORD MEANING 'SCISSORS'!

BURROWERS

The SNAKEHEAD looks as it sounds. It will attack anything that moves when it's breeding. Unlike most fish it can breathe air and survive for several hours out of water (even longer if it burrows into mud).

STINGERS

GIANT FRESHWATER STINGRAYS can grow to 5m long and weigh more than 8 times an average adult human! The stingray has a poisonous barb at the base of its tail. It rarely attacks people but has been known to overturn boats.

POUNCERS

TIGERFISH are the piranhas of Africa. Ferocious predators, they have been known to jump out of the water and catch birds in flight.

BLINDING BUGS

RIVER BLINDNESS is a nasty disease. It's not caused by a river itself, but by tiny blackflies that live in tropical waters. First they bite you, then they squirt in little grubs that grow into harmful worms inside your body.

HUNTERS

BULL SHARKS have a reputation for danger and are found in both fresh and saltwater. During floods in Queensland, Australia in 2010/11, several were seen swimming in the streets.

Who uses rivers as roads?

A dugout canoe on the Amazon

They may not have traffic lights or zebra crossings, but rivers can act a lot like roads. Boats chug up and down waterways around the world, carrying people and cargo. Rivers can mark borders between different countries – AND make handy links between them.

THE DANUBE IS THE SECOND-LONGEST RIVER IN EUROPE (THE VOLGA IN RUSSIA TAKES FIRST PRIZE)!

The Danube in Europe is the world's most international river. It flows through or borders 10 countries, and its basin extends into 9 more. Starting as a spring in the Black Forest of Germany, it snakes its way to the Romanian Black Sea past a string of famous cities and fortresses.

The Danube has long been an important trade route, big enough for ocean-going ships to power along it. Now it connects all the way to the Atlantic, thanks to a canal that joins it to the rivers Main and Rhine.

PASSENGER FERRY

Also known as a river tram, water taxi, or vaporetto (if you happen to be in Venice), a ferry is one way to get from A to B if you're sick of buses.

DUGOUT CANOE

Deep in the Amazon, a canoe is a handy way to get to school.

ANCIENT BORDERS

Rivers once held back the Roman Empire! For 400 years, the Rhine and the Danube separated the Romans from 'barbarians' on the other side. They also let the two sides trade.

Look at a world map. Which rivers form country borders today?

• **BUILD A BRIDGE!**
Some of the longest river bridges in the world cross the Yangtze.

• **TUNNEL UNDER!**
Did you know that parts of London's Tube run under the Thames river?

CARGO BARGE

Shanghai port

This is a cheap, if slow, way to transport goods. Shanghai, at the mouth of the Yangtze river, China, is the world's busiest port. In 2013, 776 million tonnes of cargo passed through it, on more than 2,000 container ships per month.

Europe's busiest port is Rotterdam, where the Rhine meets the North Sea.

The Jiujiang River bridge over the Yangtze

MORE THAN 30 MILLION TONNES OF CARGO ARE FERRIED DOWN THE DANUBE IN A YEAR.

Where was the deadliest river flood?

Rivers have lots of uses – but they can be deadly too. The biggest killer flood was in China in 1931, when three major rivers burst their banks. Overflowing rivers still cause disasters around the world, though over the years we've got better at building flood defences.

Up to 4 million people lost their lives in 1931, when China's Yangtze, Huai and Huang He rivers flooded. Millions more families were affected as water flattened their homes. The floods happened after several years of drought, followed by torrential rains, snow and cyclones.

Today most flood-prone areas are better protected. Dams, levees and other defences have been built to hold back water, and forecasts can warn if extreme weather is on its way. Even so, riverside communities can be devastated, especially in regions that get bombarded by tropical storms.

FLOODING

Thousands of people fled their homes in Europe when the River Danube flooded in June 2013.

WARNING! LESS THAN A METRE OF FAST-FLOWING FLOODWATER CAN WASH AWAY A CAR!

Extreme measures were taken to protect this house in Mississippi!

INDIA AND BANGLADESH

In 2004, heavy monsoon rains flooded the Ganges and Brahmaputra rivers, wiping out about 8.5 MILLION homes.

*** NOT ALL BAD ***

In many regions, people rely on regular floods to sweep silt (fine, fertile soil) from the river onto their farmland. Floodplains are popular places to live, especially in developing countries.

DAM IT!

The Aswan High Dam in Egypt controls the Nile's yearly flood. The downside is that farmers now need fertilisers, because their land no longer benefits from the river's rich black mud.

RISK FACTOR

A severe flood, with a 1% chance of happening in a year, is called a 100-year flood. A 50-year flood has a 2% chance of occurring, and so on.

MISSISSIPPI

In 2011, parts of the Mississippi spilt over after heavy rains and snowmelt. The flooding affected:

- more than 21,000 homes and businesses
- nearly 5,000 square kilometres of farmland
- about 43,000 people

Damage costs reached US$2.8 billion.

How can rivers light up houses?

Every time you watch TV, boil a kettle, charge your phone or switch on a light, you're using electricity. But did you know that nearly a fifth of the electricity used in the world today comes from hydropower – in other words, the power of rushing water?

AT LEAST 150 COUNTRIES USE HYDROPOWER!

The famous Hoover Dam near Las Vegas, America.

NOTES ON ENERGY

MODERN WONDER

Itaipu Dam in Brazil/Paraguay has been named as one of the Wonders of the Modern World – along with the Channel Tunnel!

If you've ever seen whitewater rafting, you'll know how powerful rivers can be! Hydroelectric systems harness that power and turn it into energy we can use. Once a hydro plant is built, it provides a cheap, clean and renewable source of electricity – after all, river and rainwater comes for free.

A typical hydro plant starts with a dam, with water stored behind it in a reservoir. Opening the dam sends water rushing over turbines inside, which turn as the water pushes at them. The turbines spin a generator to make electricity.

TO DAM...

China's Three Gorges Dam is the biggest hydro plant in the world. Built on the Yangtze river, it can generate as much electricity as 15 nuclear power stations and supply more than 50 million homes.

When the people of Shanghai turn on their lights, they can thank the Yangtze river!

OR NOT TO DAM

Dams can be controversial because to build them, you have to drown a lot of land. The Three Gorges project wiped out 13 cities, 140 towns, 1,350 villages and displaced 1.2 million people. Dams also disrupt river wildlife.

WATER WHEELS

Even the Ancient Greeks used hydropower! Their water wheels had buckets that filled to make them turn. This could drive a mill to grind flour.

'Hydro' is the Greek word for water.

MICRO

If you live near a steep stream or river, you can make your own hydropower! Micro-hydro systems use the natural flow of water to power single homes or small communities.

It takes a massive amount of energy to light up a big city like Shanghai

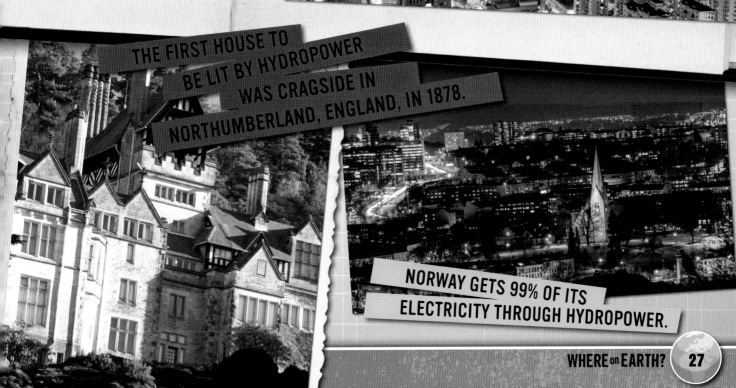

THE FIRST HOUSE TO BE LIT BY HYDROPOWER WAS CRAGSIDE IN NORTHUMBERLAND, ENGLAND, IN 1878.

NORWAY GETS 99% OF ITS ELECTRICITY THROUGH HYDROPOWER.

Can rivers turn to ice?

Running water takes a lot longer to freeze than still water. But in the depths of winter, small rivers and streams can freeze. Even if they don't turn completely solid, some rivers freeze enough to be used as roads.

The Arctic has some of the world's biggest rivers. In chilly Siberia, Russia, rivers can be frozen along their whole length for 70 to 250 days in a year. The Ob-Irtysh ices over for up to six months from October to April, then creeps slowly back to life when the weather warms.

Some rivers just freeze in parts, or seal over with an icy crust on top. 'Ice jams' can happen when frozen sections block the flow of water behind them, causing flooding. There's also a big flood risk when the ice starts to break up or melt, releasing sudden torrents of water.

The big freeze! Sheet ice covers the Susquehanna river at Harrisburg, Pennsylvania, USA

THE LONGER A RIVER IS FROZEN, THE THICKER THE ICE BECOMES!

NOTES ON ICE

>>ICE ROADS<<

Some frozen rivers could take the weight of an elephant. Others get so iced up they become roads! At certain times of year you can drive on:

- The Tana, Norway
- The Lena, Russia
- The Mackenzie, Canada.

Ice roads have strict speed and weight limits and vehicles aren't allowed to stop.

FROST FAIR

England's River Thames used to freeze so heavily that Frost Fairs were held on it. A cross between a Christmas market and a funfair, the last one was in 1814.

ICE BOATS

When the US Hudson river freezes over, ice yacht racers bring out their tobogganing boats!

THIN ICE

Frozen rivers are changing with the climate. Scientists found that the Lena river's ice thinned by 73cm from 1955-2012.

COLD CLIMB

Even waterfalls can freeze up for part of the year. Good news for crazy climbers.

BLAST IT

At the end of each winter, specialists in Ottawa, Canada, bomb its frozen rivers to break the ice and stop meltwater flooding the city.

IN 2012, AN UNEXPECTED FREEZE DISRUPTED SHIPPING TRAFFIC ON THE DANUBE.

What on Earth? words

aquifer an underground layer of rock that water can sink into or pass through

canal a human-made channel of water

canyon a deep hollow in the landscape, usually with a river running through it

cargo goods carried on a ship or other vehicle

current a flow of water in one direction

cyclone a tropical storm

dam a wall built to hold back water, usually to prevent flooding or produce hydropower

delta an area of flat land, built up by a river at its mouth

drought a long period of low rainfall

ecosystem a community of living things in a particular environment

erosion the wearing away of land by water, wind or other natural processes

evaporate to turn from liquid to vapour, or gas

floodplain the low-lying land on either side of a river

fresh water water that's not salty, including water in rivers, lakes and streams

glacier a slow-moving river of ice, found on high mountains and near the Poles

groundwater water held underground in the soil or rock

irrigate to supply water to farmland, especially to help crops grow

levee an embankment built to prevent a river overflowing

meander a bend in a winding river

monsoon rains very heavy rains that come seasonally in southern Asia

mouth where a river flows into a lake or the sea

predator an animal that hunts other animals for food

reservoir a human-made lake

river basin the land from which surface water drains into a river and its tributaries

source the starting point of a river, such as a lake or spring

spring a place where water flows from underground to the surface

tidal wave an exceptionally large ocean wave, for example caused by storms or earthquakes

transpiration the process whereby a plant takes in water and releases water vapour

tributary a river or stream flowing into a larger river

valley a low area of land between hills or mountains, usually carved by a river

water vapour the gas formed when water evaporates

Further information

BOOKS

River Adventures: titles include *Amazon*, *Ganges*, *Mississippi*, *Nile*, *Thames*, *Yangtze* by Paul Manning, Franklin Watts, 2012–14

Journey Along the Amazon (*Travelling Wild*) by Alex Woolf, Wayland, 2014

Rivers Around the World (*Geography Now*) by Jen Green, Wayland, 2011

Raging Rivers (*Horrible Geography*) by Anita Ganeri and Mike Phillips, Scholastic, 2008

The World's Most Amazing Rivers (*Landform Top 10s*) by Anita Ganeri, Raintree, 2010

WEBSITES

http://education.nationalgeographic.co.uk/education/encyclopedia/river/?ar_a=1
All about rivers and their uses around the world.

http://www.onegeology.org/extra/kids/earthprocesses/rivers.html
Find out how a river changes along its course.

http://www.3dgeography.co.uk/#!river-facts/cfvg
Fast facts and statistics about rivers.

http://primaryfacts.com/rivers-facts-information-and-resources/
Interesting info about famous rivers.

http://education.nationalgeographic.co.uk/education/encyclopedia/waterfall/?ar_a=1
Get the low-down on waterfalls, with a case study on Niagara.

http://environment.nationalgeographic.com/environment/global-warming/hydropower-profile/
Discover the story of hydropower.

http://water.usgs.gov/edu/hyhowworks.html
Get to grips with how hydropower works.

http://www.nps.gov/grca/index.htm
The Grand Canyon National Park website.

CLIPS

https://www.youtube.com/watch?v=YSBye1LFaug
Witness Nik Wallenda's terrifying tightrope walk over Niagara Falls…

… and Will Gadd climbing UP the frozen Falls – brrrr!
https://www.youtube.com/watch?v=jU5i1WjRBhE

https://www.youtube.com/watch?v=4ZuZiLuHM1A
A surfer rides the Amazon pororoca wave.

https://www.youtube.com/watch?v=p2X4U1mQzoE
Exploring the Grand Canyon by boat and plane.

https://www.youtube.com/watch?v=uvfWiKFTces
Bombs away! Blasting the Ottawa river ice.

INDEX